God & Mambo

*truth, rhythm
and verse*

*ritmo, verdad
y verso*

Meriel Martínez

Editor for English: Nancy Stevenson
Editor for Spanish: Julia Caballero

Cover and Interior Design: Wanda España/Wee Design Group

Published by Nariad Publishing
Copyright © 2014 by Meriel Martínez

To daddy, my first inspiration.

A papi, mi primera inspiración.

contents

envisioning a joyful death 1
África 3
questions 5
Today I am USA 7
desperation 9
writer's insomnia 11
beso boricua 13
crush 15
chaos 17
train ride 19
suspiro 21
Mariposas for Paloma 23
emerge 25
Inaru la bella 27
because she knows her numbers 29
mi hija 31
Nadia-lin 33
vanity in the vanity 35
me las imagino 37
spell break 39
not the script I would have written 41
let me grieve on your behalf 43
dinosaurs 45
les miento 47
springtime 49
in summer breeze 51
te invito 53
to a love lost 55
amnesia 57
es mejor que no 59
gardens 61
malfunction 63
reclamo 65
beast 67
some days 69
love songs 71
if you ask me 73
el mambo y el tiempo 75

envisioning a joyful death

head swinging, arms rocking
chest pulsing, hips swerving
knees dipping, butt swaying
legs pumping, feet gliding

  body saturated in mambo, maybe del Gran Combo
   drenched in the singular energy of congas, timbales
    short of breath, exhausted and exhilarated
    heart pounding so, chest can't contain the thrill

     too old for this, but when the mother lands call,
     manipulate with their rhythms, YES! is all I can answer
     and if I get the final call in the middle of this joy – *Pues perfecto.* –
     at the peak of gladness, immersed in that of which I am made
     Can you show me a better way to go? I don't think so.

África

vive África en mi pecho
llevo el continente dentro
su tierra reside en mi alma
su ritmo construye mi centro

mi piel no es color café
ni rizos son mis cabellos
mi cuerpo no es Yoruba
mas Yoruba es lo que siento

los timbales me dan vida
y las congas son mi aliento
cuando suenan, en mi vientre
qué alegría experimento

cuando retumba la clave
no me queda más remedio
que olvidar lo cotidiano
y entregarme a ese momento
permitir que se apodere
de mi cada movimiento,
porque África vive en mí
como Dios vive en mis sueños

questions

There sit these questions on my chest
I wish I'd asked before you left
There live these stories in my mind
of gentler words and softer times
But I don't know if they are true,
if they are real - I wish I knew

    The childhood memories never shared
    I wonder why you never dared
    The hurt, the anger locked away,
    the desperation of your days
    You hid it all behind that smile,
    but you were drowning all the while

    I'm sure that's why you had to go,
    but I was young and didn't know
    And so these questions still remain,
    at times evoking waves of pain
    But there is hope and there is faith
    I trust you're in a better place

Today I am USA

Today I am USA
not underprivileged spic american
I am New York City
not Nuyorican
I am Washington D.C.
not woman of downtrodden colors

Today I became the Twin Towers
not tired of trying
I became the Pentagon
not pent-up anger with a gun

Today I have been bombed
I have been burned
I have been pulled apart
But I've also been fortified
I have been saved
and I have been made so proud
that I cry out loud –
Today I am USA!

desperation

no longer soothing to sob in silence
nor freeing to cry out loud
I find no pleasure in vibrant songs
and lively rhythms make me frown

the sound of my voice protesting
defending the disputable truth
that sound is now exhausting
when once it was exalting

once, it was exciting –
to make myself be heard,
to swing my hips and twirl and twirl
but now my mind is all that spins;
my voice is vile; locked are my limbs

I confess on this shred of paper
that I push joy away
for I'm afraid to let it stay,
that I choose the constancy of pain
over the whim of cheerful days

writer's insomnia

it's late at night
I'm forced to write
I want to sleep
but cannot fight
this nervous urge
insistent surge
the ink stains deep
my thoughts I purge

I never know
what words will flow
if them I'll keep
or let them go

......

it's just a high
the words run dry
no longer creep
invade my mind

muse off my chest
now I can rest
for peaceful sleep
renew my quest

......

it's all in vain
the need remains
once more rhymes leap
swell in my brain

it starts again
pick up the pen
this climb so steep
concedes no end

beso boricua

no existe en mi corazón
cosita más deliciosa
que un beso sabrosón
de tu bella y rica boca

ni flan de dulce coco
ni alcapurrias ni mofongo
ni un pollo bien asao
ni tostones ni pegao

ni piragua al medio día
ni una limonada fría
ni tampoco un buen lechón
servido con chicharrón

ni viandas con bacalao
ni sopita con salchichón
ni arrocito con gandules
derechito del fogón

sabrosura no hay mejor
que uno de esos besitos
más aún si me lo das
bajo el sol de Puerto Rico

crush

I desperately long to kiss him
softly, perfectly
on the full of his lips

To weave him a song
and carve him a dance
To sing him a dawn
and dance him a sunset

I desperately want to kiss him
lightly, barely
on the plush of his lips

chaos

complex and transparent
naïve and aware
certain and doubtful
fearless and scared

  response with no question
  void overflowing
    thirst made of liquid
      wisdom not knowing

        joyful and painful
        jagged and smooth
          carefree and stunted
          brand new and used

          stillness in motion
          spark with no flair
          secret announcement
          chains made of air

train ride

confident stride
nothing to hide
handsome faces
 pose in all places

  pitiful sight
   looking to fight
    cut-up faces
     bleed from all places

      best-selling books
      well-sharpened knives
      both for survival
      on the train ride

       don't graze my hand
       or stand too close by
       unless you want problems
       on the train ride

suspiro

   espero en las tinieblas
   sudando
   escucho mi respiración
    fuerte, densa
     el suspiro del miedo
      igual al del placer
       incontrolables
        las palpitaciones del corazón
         el terror y el amor
          hermanos, cómplices

Mariposas for Paloma

those jumping, lilting things
with multicolor wings
are fluttering deep inside
are hoping to take flight

  they know she wants to sing
   let inspiration in
    and one by one they'll flow
    up to that place they know
    and as they rise become
    skilled dancers on her tongue

      the words she's often sung
      to please her God, the One
      she offers now once more
      and faithfully they soar

      winged melodies from above
      spring forward from a dove

emerge

I want her to emerge
from this bleak hole
      this   hole
her   bleak hole

I want her to emerge
      bright
        shining
like tear-filled eyes

And they are tears of joy
because she will emerge
like a tidal wave
    a   wave
her   tidal wave
  of dreams

Inaru la bella

Inaru la bella se duerme en mi pecho
Me fijo en su rostro tan dulce y tan tierno

Sus ojos chinitos cuando están despiertos
parecen dos lunas con el sol por dentro

Mas sus cachetotes que siguen creciendo
son dos panes dulces de comerse a besos

Y cuando angelitos visitan sus sueños
se llenan de risa sus labios perfectos

Inaru la bella suspira en mi pecho
Su cara bonita se parece al cielo

because she knows her numbers

because she knows her numbers
and her colors too
she wants to show me
how much she's learned
how much she's grown
what she can do

   her tiny hand, a wobbly trace
    the look of triumph on her face
     the hearts and flowers in red and blue
    "I love you" scribbled, a rosy hue

     because she knows her letters
     and her prayers too
     she wants to show me
     how much she knows…
     she doesn't know
     I'm learning too

mi hija

Mi hija
me inspira con esos ojos alegres
su mirada me dice —Te amo
me anuncia —Soy feliz
y con eso me da las gracias

Pero las gracias se las debo yo
a ella y a Dios
porque la amo
porque es mi felicidad

Mi princesa,
mi hada sonriente
brilla
como las estrellas
que admira de noche
como el sol
que busca en las mañanas

Nadia-lin

mi Nadia-lin
mi Nadia-lú
eres mi todo
eso eres tú

monstruito rosado
tormenta bestial
aterciopelada
de lindo rosal

Nadia-lu-lú
Nadia-lin-lin
mi reto diario
traviesa sin fin

mi niña mimada
repleta de vida
mi negrita china
mi chiquitirina

Nadia-sin-lin
Nadia-su-lú
vienes directa
del cielo azul

vanity in the vanity

my morning blindness can't disguise
these dirty little aging lines
keep popping up around my eyes
can't seem to help but multiply

  by golden rule do I abide
   I gently pat as I apply
    but lotions potions are a lie
     moist myths sure to dissatisfy

      and let's not talk about the gray
      I won't forget that dreadful day
      when to my uttermost dismay
      unto my crown they made their way

      so my reflection has betrayed
      my faith in youth that never strays
      since outward signs won't be delayed
     another view I will embrace
     I'll simply learn to celebrate
    the wisdom that will come with age

me las imagino

me las imagino
caminando de brazo en brazo
la brisa del mar
hace caracoles de sus cabellos

   huellas de sus piececitos
    impresas en la arena
     prueba de que existe la inocencia

      me las imagino
      corriendo hacia los brazos de papá
      la risa sin parar
      hace mariposas de sus sonrisas

      huellas de sus besitos
      impresas en el alma
      prueba de que existe la dulzura

     me las imagino
     durmiendo entre mis brazos
     las niñas de rosal
     hacen realidades mis ensueños

  huellas de sus manitos
impresas en mi pecho
prueba de que existe el consuelo

spell break

I want to break the spell
pretense of married bliss
the hurt of every spiteful act
suppressed with every kiss

  the fists composed of words
  the blows made of neglect
    the strain of always wondering
    what cruelty would come next

      of what would he accuse
      unlikely plot suspect
      what kindness view with threatened eyes
      and forcefully reject

      I plan to break the spell
      construct my happiness
      and with my angels by my side
      move forward, no regrets

not the script I would have written

not the script I would have written
got the lead without audition
forced to play the wrong rendition of my life

  can't escape this stage I live in
    too-bright lights and musty curtains
      have to bear both mask and burden as if fine

        other scenes I would have chosen
          ones with colored beats to soak in
            but instead the notes are broken, sad and vile

              trusted lines when I was younger
              became lies spit out by hunger
              but the show, majestic blunder, must go on

let me grieve on your behalf

let me grieve on your behalf
commit yourself to joy
I can persuade the painful path
  to let you through without a scratch

  let me lament the sorrows past
    the split-up birthdays
      the unshared laughs
        the Christmas mornings with missing halves

      let me wallow in your stead
        assign yourself to peace
        I will convince the lingering dread
        to step aside and let you breathe

dinosaurs

Mommy! – my little one said,
as she sprang from her colorful bed –
There are dinosaurs inside my head!

I keep yelling at them: Go away!
but they brush off what I have to say
and just roar in my mind anyway!

Every night they return
when the sky has gone gray
and I run, run away
But they still stomp their way
to the top of the stairs
through the door, to my bed,
and straight into my head!

Those dinosaurs, mommy,
my little one said,
look like running too late,
like no treat after dinner
like those games that I hate
because I'm not the winner

like my sister, the swiper
who still wears icky diapers
like my face with these rashes
that get worse if I scratch them

like my heart that divides
each time I say goodbye
daddy's turn to play ghost
mommy's turn to serve dinner
and this game I hate most
because no one's the winner

les miento

les miento
les digo que no tienen de qué preocuparse
que todo saldrá bien
que el sol nunca para de brillar y
que la luna siempre será su guía
que solo hace falta contar con Dios, y con su madre

mientras, yo sí me preocupo
y sé que las cosas a veces van muy mal
he visto cuando el sol se enoja y desaparece
y cuando la luna se cansa y se esconde

sin embargo, insisto en que siempre deben contar
con Dios y con su madre,
porque Dios es amor y yo su cómplice

springtime

piles of snow swallow the ground
winds punish worn trees and old limbs
a swelling, familiar, possesses the clouds
ice pellets choose targets at whim

  with shovel in tow
   I push through again
    a dull, stunted spirit
     soul aching for spring
      take rest for a moment
     look up and I see
      my vibrant sunflowers
      smile sweetly at me

     in that honest moment
     the cold disappears
     no heartache, no worries, no sorrow, no fears
     for bright-colored flowers
     with eyes vivid brown
    shine sunlight eternal
   line silver the clouds

  blankets of snow still pile on the ground
 winds sting as they steadily climb
but I'm warm and I'm light and I simply don't mind
'cause my springtime is waiting inside

in summer breeze

in summer breeze
or winter snow
it's just the same
i love you so

  on leafy paths of fall
   we'll prance
     amidst the dawn of spring
    we'll dance

     in north and south
     and all the rest
     you are my joy
     my happiness

te invito

Te invito a olvidarte del pasado
a unirte al presente
a imaginarte el futuro

Te reto a abandonar la incertidumbre
a lanzarte en aguas frías
a creer en la esperanza

Te llamo a reírte sin motivo
a sentir lo invisible
a refugiarte en la belleza

Atrévete. Vive. Ama.

to a love lost

The extent to which I love you
is a truly marvelous thing
It would circle all the planets
if it turned into a string

If a warrior it became
all the world would know her name
History books could not contain her
bravery, honor, without stain

If it grew into a tree
oh how luscious it would be
bearing fruits of such delight
unmatched joy in every bite

If a river it should be
it would beckon: Follow me.
Show itself in all its forms
rapid, tranquil, cool and warm

The extent to which I love you
you may never comprehend
It's a thing of strength and wonder
knows no boundaries, has no end

amnesia

you should know that I love you still
but don't know how much more I will

   from broken hearts seep many things
    like dreams of bliss and wedding rings

   though now you occupy this space
    someday another will replace

      from shattered hopes burst many things
      like soul grenades and fears that swing

      today I know who this is for
      this time next year I'll know no more

es mejor que no

es mejor que no
me reconozcas
ni me vengas a saludar
no quiero recordar lo pasado
o pretender que existe un futuro

   es mejor que no
     bailemos como antes, tan cerca
     mejor si nos quedamos
     tranquilos, sin hablar
     ni mirar, ni tocar

       es mejor que no
       me des un beso en la mejilla
       ni en cualquier otro lugar
       ni el cabello me debes rozar
       no, es mejor que no
       adiós

gardens

gardens in bloom he promised
and ever-fertile land
but now it seems that I must sow
this patch with my own hand

  so many nights he spoke to me
   of truth and strength and love
    but they turned out to be the things
    that he knew nothing of

      another time I've watched him go
      rush down a separate path
      but I'll stand still and, if it will,
      let love find its way back

malfunction

your heart, not mine, is ill-equipped
mine's fueled by blood, yours by a chip
mine can survive a nuclear blast
yours self-destructs from just one scratch

  I thought your zest arose with ease
   not run by cranks behind the scenes
    consistent thumps I heard as beats
     were measured clanks from your machine

      had I known yours was poorly made
      with faulty parts that rust and fade
      I might have guessed the thing would wear
      eject its core without a care

      but in no way could I have seen
      the muck that sat behind your sheen
      you hid it well, so I believed
      your heart, like mine, was evergreen

reclamo

Reclamo mi derecho
a ser mujer
a sentir
deseo ternura pasión

  a permitir que mis caderas
   hablen por mí
    que mis muslos
     den un discurso
    y mis brazos
     una lección

      Reclamo mi derecho
      a ser compleja
      contradictoria
      madre amante intelectual
      dulzura ardor coraje
      a dar caricias de caramelo
      y besos de sal y limón

  Me reclamo a mí misma
  a todo lo que he sido, soy y seré

beast

wise it had been to let her be
to let her rest so peacefully
her body calm, her senses weak

 before, she simmered at low heat
 one word from you and up she peaked
  and now there's steam, up rises steam

   might've been best to let her sleep
    the force that stirs inside of me
   awaiting you, accosting me

     and now, awake, she beckons me
     relentlessly, no rest, no sleep
     tormented by her fantasy in which on you she feasts

some days

some days
it's already there when you wake
this deep warmth, this heat, pouring from your breast
a force you can't disguise, control or contain

  it heaves, your chest, as you picture him
   his luscious skin, like chocolate
    sculpted to edible perfection
     or maybe caramel, drizzling where it will

      it waters, your mouth, as you drown in him
      strong arms that take you in, captive
      collapsing under his imposing will
      you willed it to be so

      often
      you delight in this ardent pleasure
      his want, pulsating through your every inch
      a force only he can ignite, extinguish, and start
      again

love songs

he's got me singing love songs
the most demented kind
the ones where everything is swell
and all the stars align

  those songs where dancing is required
   with flawless choreography
    where lovers glide with beaming smiles
    and hit their mark on every beat

     you know those songs where we're all one
      a single earthly family
      where strangers join and dance along
      and all can sing on perfect key

     indeed, it is those love songs
     the most outrageous kind
     ones far removed from what is real
    that in my heart reside
    and he's to blame, you know his name
   the one who claims he's mine

if you ask me

if you ask me, I'll say yes
I don't need the long, white dress
or the fifteen hundred guests

we can skip the drawn-out plans
seating charts in sweaty hands
choosing cutlery and a band

let's forget the fancy hall
winding stairs and mirrored walls
chandeliers that just might fall

if you ask me, I'll ask when
doesn't suit me to pretend
it can wait until year's end

checked-off lists of pros and cons
we've been keeping all along
can restrain us but so long

all the math it has been done
one plus one has just one sum
here we go and here we come

el mambo y el tiempo

el mambo y el tiempo
todo lo curan
el primero te alegra
el segundo perdura
más allá del dolor

el mambo conoce
muy bien tu aflicción
recluta la clave
timbales, tambor
y sana la herida
con puro sabor

el tiempo percibe
tu necesidad
te espera tranquilo
te ayuda a alcanzar
los dulces momentos
de felicidad

el tiempo y el mambo
todo lo resuelven
son amigos constantes
que al sufrir desenvuelven
y así mismo convierten
a la pena en amor

www.ingramcontent.com/pod-product-compliance
Lightning Source LLC
Chambersburg PA
CBHW071408040426
42444CB00009B/2148